Mega and Big Dash

Written by Catherine Baker

Illustrated by Pipi Sposito

Collins

1 The boss

What is that on the shed?

Check me out – I am MEGA SLUG!

Mega Slug is the boss of the allotment.

rush

dash

Mega Slug gets rid of pests.

I do not munch carrots and pumpkins ...

I like chips!

Big Dash is the BIGGEST pest on the allotment.

Big Dash can crunch carrots.

He can munch pumpkins.

He can chomp this mega-radish as well!

I must get rid of Big Dash!

2 Bad plans ...

Mega Slug has a plan.

I will fix a trap!

trap full of mush

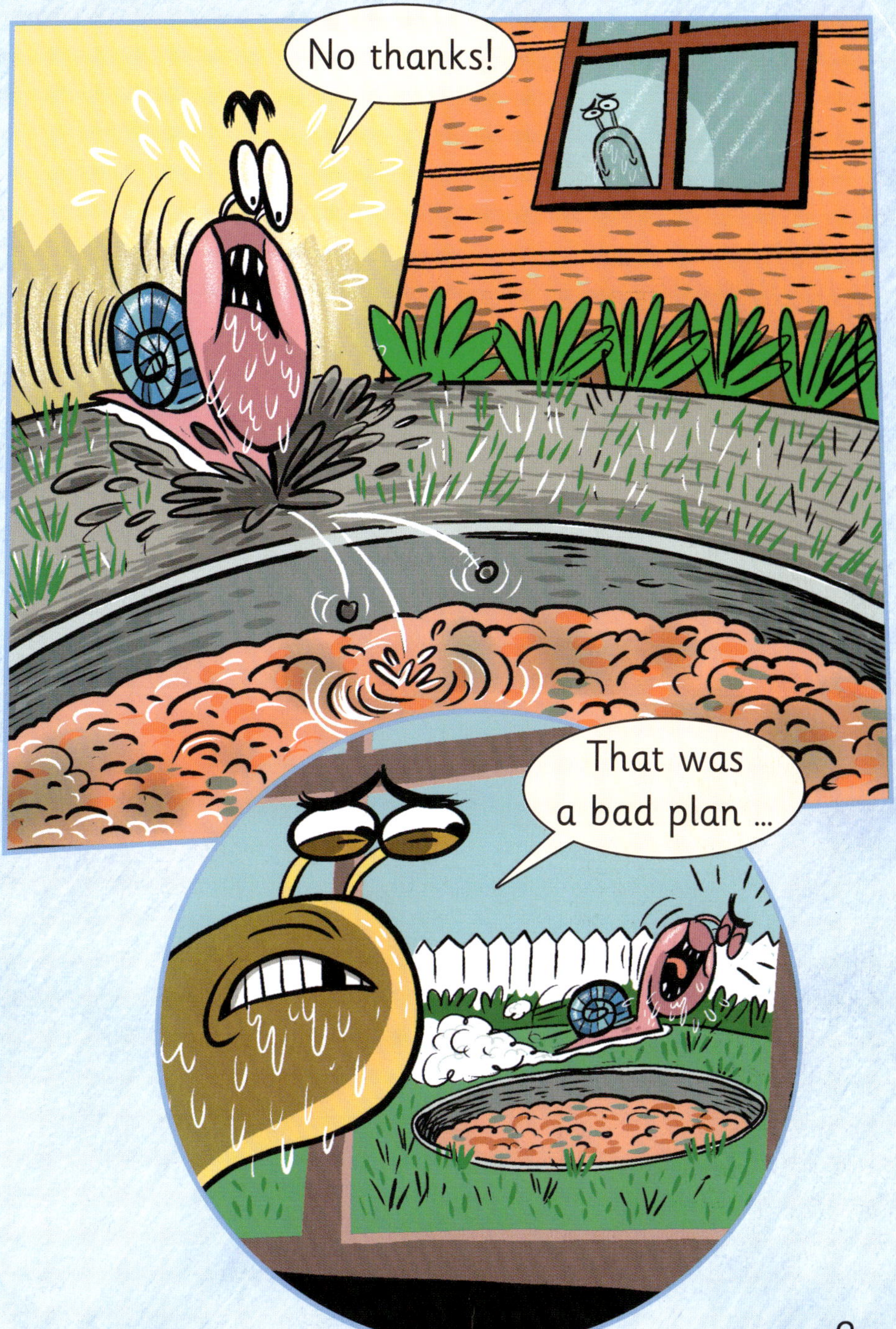
No thanks!
That was a bad plan ...

I will jump on his shell! He will get a shock and dash off!

jump

crash

That was a bad plan as well.

I will stash all the carrots in the shed.

vanish

"Big Dash will quit this allotment!"

full shed

13

But that is a mega-bad plan!

No pumpkins ...

not one radish ...

and no carrots!

Drat that pest!

3 The best trick

Mega Slug has a mega-think.

think ...

think ...

16

think ...

I will trick Big Dash – with this track!
Biggest Carrots on this track!

I am the biggest pest, so I will munch the biggest carrots!
rush
dash

Big Dash slips in the mud ...

crunch

bash

19

Big Dash ends up at the bottom of the hill.

Mega Slug locks him out.

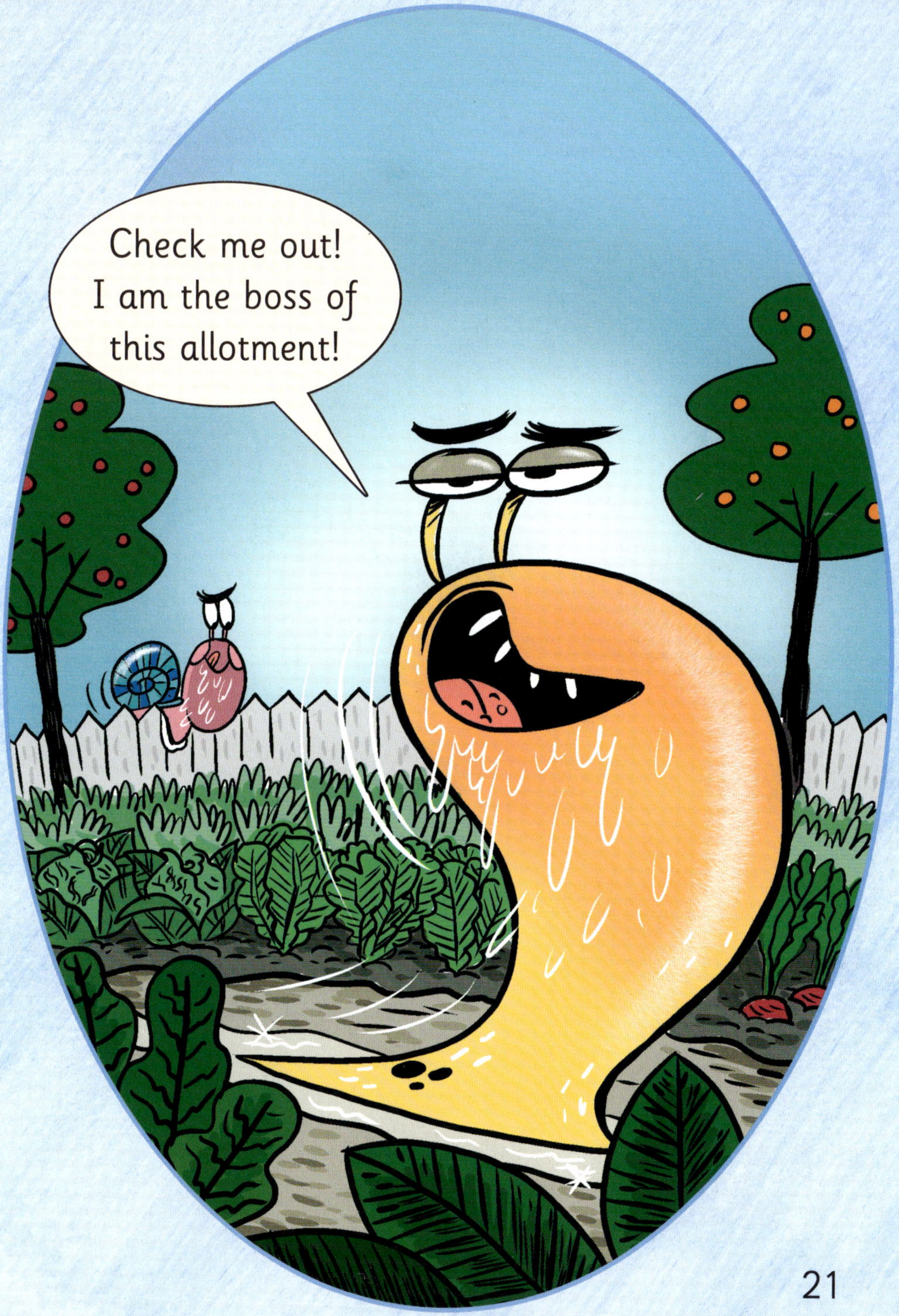
Check me out!
I am the boss of
this allotment!

Finish Mega Slug's track

23

After reading

Letters and Sounds: Phases 3 and 4
Word count: 234
Focus phonemes: /ch/ /sh/ /th/, and adjacent consonants
Common exception words: of, the, no, I, all, full, he, was, like, so, do, out, what, me, one
Curriculum links: Science: Animals, including humans
National Curriculum learning objectives: Reading/word reading: apply phonic knowledge and skills as the route to decode words; read accurately by blending sounds in unfamiliar words containing GPCs that have been taught; Reading/comprehension (KS2): understand what they read, in books they can read independently, by checking that the text makes sense to them, discussing their understanding and explaining the meaning of words in context; discussing words and phrases that capture the reader's interest and imagination; identifying how language, structure, and presentation contribute to meaning

Developing fluency

- Read the book with your child, taking it in turns to read the narration and Mega Slug's spoken words.
- Demonstrate reading with dramatic expression to bring out the humour.

Phonic practice

- Practise reading words that contain the phonemes /ch/ and /sh/.
  - Turn to page 6 and point to **crunch**. Ask your child to sound out and blend. (/c/ /r/ /u/ /n/ /ch/)
  - Then ask them to sound out and blend the following words: page 7: chomp (/ch/ /o/ /m/ /p/)   page 12: stash (/s/ /t/ /a/ /sh/)

Extending vocabulary

- Focus on the meaning of colloquial terms. Ask your child to suggest words with a similar meaning to these:
  page 8: mush (e.g. *slop, mulch*)   page 13: quit (e.g. *leave, exit*)
  page 15: drat (e.g. *bother, rats*)
  page 14: mega-bad (e.g. *terrible, unbelievably awful*)
- Ask your child to check the context to see if their favourite alternative word makes sense.